Titles in the series

A SNOWY DAY   WHAT CAN I HEAR?
A STORMY DAY   WHAT CAN I SEE?
A SUNNY DAY   WHAT CAN I TASTE?
A WINDY DAY   WHAT CAN I TOUCH?

CLEAN AND DIRTY   COTTON
HOT AND COLD   GLASS
LIGHT AND DARK   RUBBER
WET AND DRY   WOOD

BEANS
BREAD
FRUIT
VEGETABLES

British Library Cataloguing in Publication Data

Petty, Kate
Cotton.
1. Cotton
I. Title   II. Baker, Madeleine   III. Series
677'.21
ISBN 0-340-50389-0

First published 1990

Published by Hodder and Stoughton Children's Books,
a division of Hodder and Stoughton Ltd,
Mill Road, Dunton Green, Sevenoaks, Kent TN13 2YA

Printed in Italy

COTTON

Kate Petty

Illustrated by Madeleine Baker

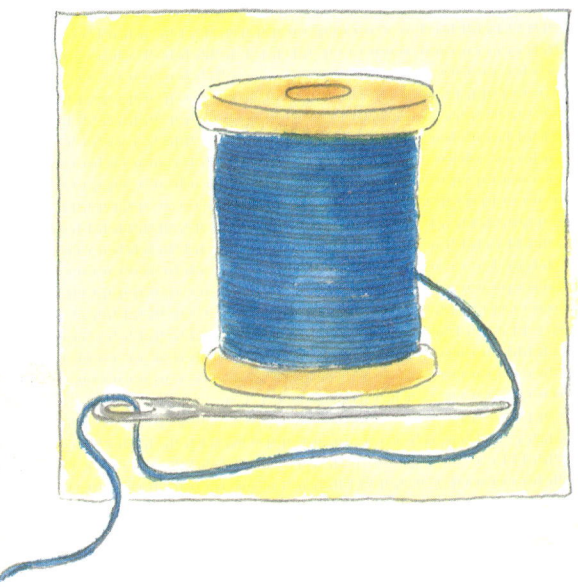

HODDER AND STOUGHTON
LONDON SYDNEY AUCKLAND TORONTO

Sanjay and his Grandma are both wearing their most comfortable clothes.

Sanjay's jeans and T-shirt, and Grandma's sari, are all made from cotton.

Materials like cotton, wool and nylon are called textiles.

flower

seed pod

cotton boll

Cotton comes from the seed pod
of the cotton plant. It needs
plenty of sunshine to grow.
Each seed is attached to a tuft
of cotton.

The fluffy seed pods – or
bolls – are picked and the seeds
taken out. The cotton is baled
up, ready to be made into cloth.

How can fleecy cotton fibres
be spun into 'yarn'?

Try pulling and twisting some
cotton wool between your
finger and thumb to see how it
can be done.

In a cotton mill the fibres
are flattened and combed and
cut into strips.

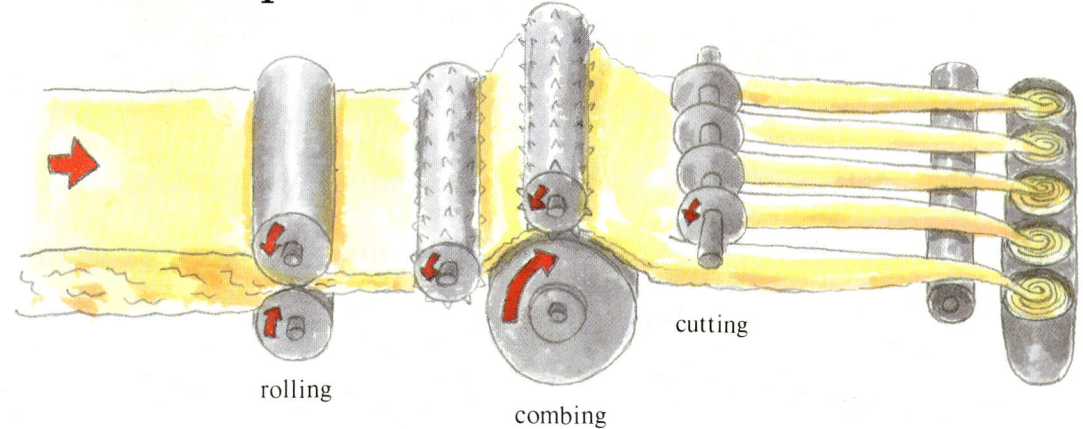

rolling

combing

cutting

Then the machines can spin
hundreds of balls of yarn at
a time.

Some yarn is knitted into cloth.
T-shirts are knitted cotton.

Most cloth is woven. These
huge automatic looms weave
blue denim from indigo-dyed
yarn.

Hand-weaving is fun.
You need: an old Christmas card
a ball of yarn 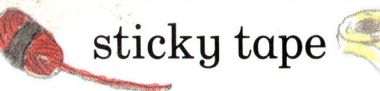 sticky tape

1. Use the card to make a loom and shuttle.

2. Set up the long threads (warp). Tape the ends to the back of the loom.

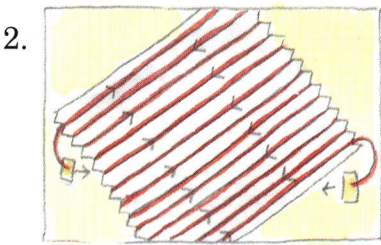

3. Use the shuttle to weave the yarn under and over the warp threads. On the way back, go over the threads you went under before, and vice versa.

4. Push the rows (weft) close together as your weaving grows.

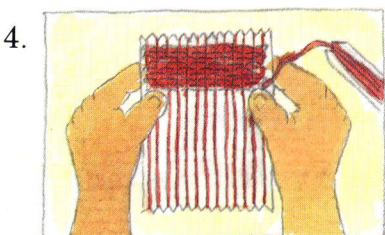

The patterns on Grandma's
sari were printed after the
cloth was woven.

Sanjay and his friends are
printing club T-shirts.

They use: a plain T-shirt
fabric paint   a paint brush
the lid from a plastic tub
thick card

1. They put newspaper on the table and inside the T-shirt.

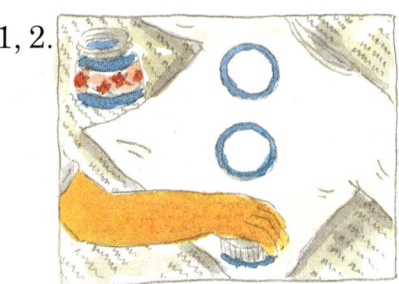

2. They paint the rim of the lid and print wheel shapes.

3. They paint a strip of thick card and print the spokes.

4. They let the picture dry. Then they iron and wash the T-shirt according to the instructions on the fabric paint.

More clothes are made with
cotton than with any other
material. It feels nice
against the skin.

Some materials make
Sanjay hot and itchy.
Cotton is cool to wear.

'Let's look at that knee.'
Poor Sanjay. Cotton wool
and bandages are made
from cotton.

Cotton is used in hospitals
for gowns and aprons, too.
Cotton can be boiled to kill
any germs.

Sanjay helps to sort the laundry. Cotton clothes can be washed at a high temperature, so all the dirt comes out.

Sanjay reads the labels.
Clothes made from a
mixture of cotton and
another material need a
cooler wash.

100% cotton

[symbol 95°] hot wash   [tumble symbol] tumble dry low

[triangle symbol] bleach   [iron symbol] iron

75%
25%   COTTON
POLYESTER

[symbol 40°] warm wash   [circle symbol] tumble dry low
[crossed symbol] no bleach   [crossed iron symbol] do not iron

While Grandma buys cotton
thread to mend his jeans,
Sanjay looks at the different
rolls of cotton.

voile

canvas

lawn

poplin

gingham

Cotton voile is fine enough to
see through. Canvas is thick
enough to make a tent. The
cottons all have different names.

Grandma sews the patch in place before she stitches it with the sewing machine.

Mum gives Sanjay his bath.
His face flannel and bath
towel are made from cotton
towelling. Cotton soaks up water.

Sanjay's special duvet cover
and pillowcase are made
from cotton. So Sanjay is
comfortable all night, too.

There are at least 23 things in this picture made from cotton. Can you spot them all? The answers are on the opposite page.

Answers:
baby's hat, bandage, bedlinen, blouse, bunting, cloth bricks, cloth rattles, cotton blanket, fancy dress, flag, flannels, rag books, rag dolls, sari, shorts, socks, sunshade, tablecloths, T-shirts, tea towel, tent, trousers, uniforms.

cotton words

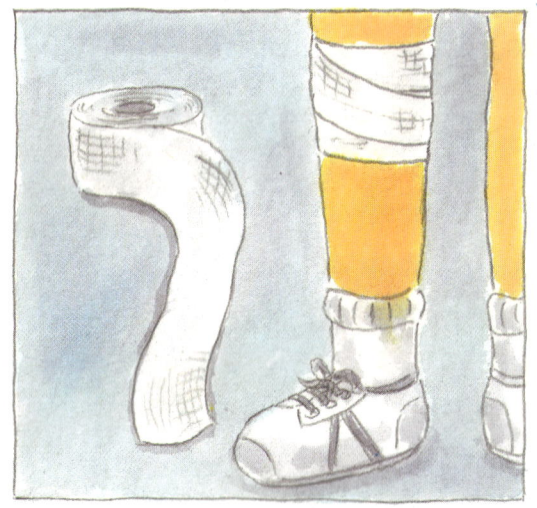

bandages

boll

cotton fabrics

knitted cotton

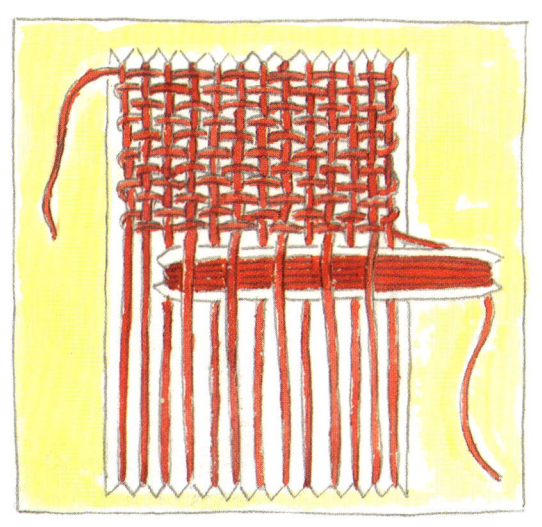

loom

sewing thread

sewing machine

towelling

25